Sisters

Venus & Serena Williams

A biography by

Jeanette Winter

Beach Lane Books   New York   London   Toronto   Sydney   New Delhi

Venus Ebony Starr Williams
and
Serena Jameka Williams
are the youngest sisters
in a family of five girls
and a mother and a father.

Venus reads to her little sister, Serena,
as night slips down over the bed they share
in their house in Compton, California.

Outside in the darkness, life goes on till early dawn,

when the sun rises up over the sisters' sleepy bed.

Daddy and Mama want their two youngest
girls to learn tennis.

They have dreams for their future.

Daddy and Mama even learn to play tennis
so they can teach Venus and Serena to play.

Early morning, Daddy takes the sisters to the court,
where some older boys still think it's night.

Daddy tells the boys his girls need to practice their tennis. Scowl meets scowl.

The morning clean-up happens,
again,
and again.
And then the practice,
with used-up balls,
not much bounce,
and used-up rackets,
not much spring.
"I didn't grow up playing
at the country club," Serena says.

Serve, return, volley,

forehand, backhand,

over and over.

"Concentrate," Daddy says.

Thwonk,

thwonk,

thwack,

back and forth, back and forth,
two little sisters learning the game.

Venus and Serena concentrate HARD,
trying not to hear the gunfire down the street.

Like in a cocoon, the sisters focus on the ball.

The boys start hanging around, watching.

The sisters have their attention. And respect.
Venus and Serena hit the ball so hard and fast
that the boys cheer them on—
and protect them.

Practice over, in the dimming light
Daddy and the little sisters go home
to Mama and their big sisters.

"Do your schoolwork, Venus.
Do your schoolwork, Serena.
I want you girls to be educated," Mama says.

The sisters listen, study, and concentrate.

"When Venus laughs, I laugh harder.

"When Venus cries, I cry harder," Serena says.

That's just how close those sisters are.

Word gets around—
about how those Williams sisters can hit that tennis ball.
Offers to give the sisters new tennis balls, new rackets,
new tennis clothes, and chances to play tennis matches
arrive at the house in Compton.

Mama braids Venus's hair for her first tournament.

When Venus walks out onto the perfect green court, she sees a sea of white faces.

Concentrate, she tells herself.

The crowd fades away, like the gunfire in Compton.
She hits the ball HARD—

Venus wins.

Then Serena plays her first tournament, white beads gleaming.
Venus cheers from the stands.

Concentrate, Serena tells herself,
and the crowd fades away.
She hits the ball HARD, back and forth—

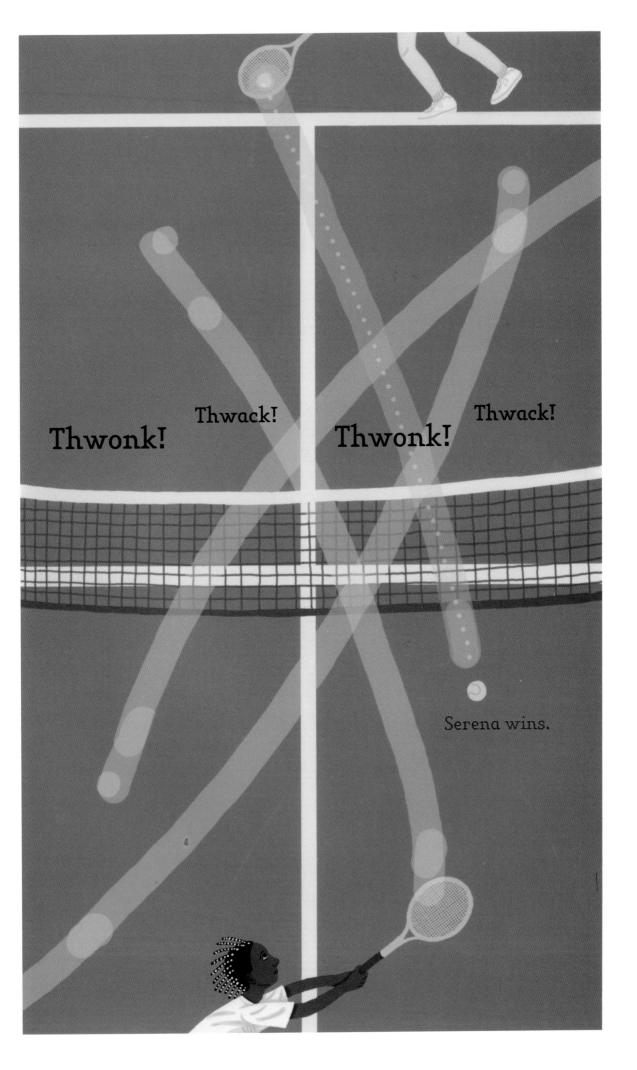

Thwonk!

Thwack!

Thwonk!

Thwack!

Serena wins.

Their trophy collection begins.

Word gets around—
a tennis academy invites the sisters
and their family to Florida.
Venus and Serena practice under palm trees,
and go to school, and practice
and go to school,

until Mama and Daddy say they are old enough
to play in the Big Tournaments.

No longer "little" sisters, Venus and Serena are tall and strong.

And they PLAY strong!

Trophies pile up—
one after another.

Trophies make some people green with envy.
But the sisters concentrate. Not hearing the
boos, they keep on winning.
They are POWERFUL!

The sisters try new ways of dressing and new hairstyles
no one has seen on a tennis court before.

Venus starts a business and designs tennis clothes,
and still plays tennis.

Serena acts on TV
and still plays tennis.

But anyone can get sick.

Venus gets a disease that makes her weak,
too weak to play tennis.
She fights to recover and play again.

Serena gets a blood clot in her lungs.
She fights to recover and play again.

The sisters train hard and practice hard
and hit those bright balls
on their own tennis court—concentrating like
they did when they were little.

And they continue to play and win,
one trophy after another.

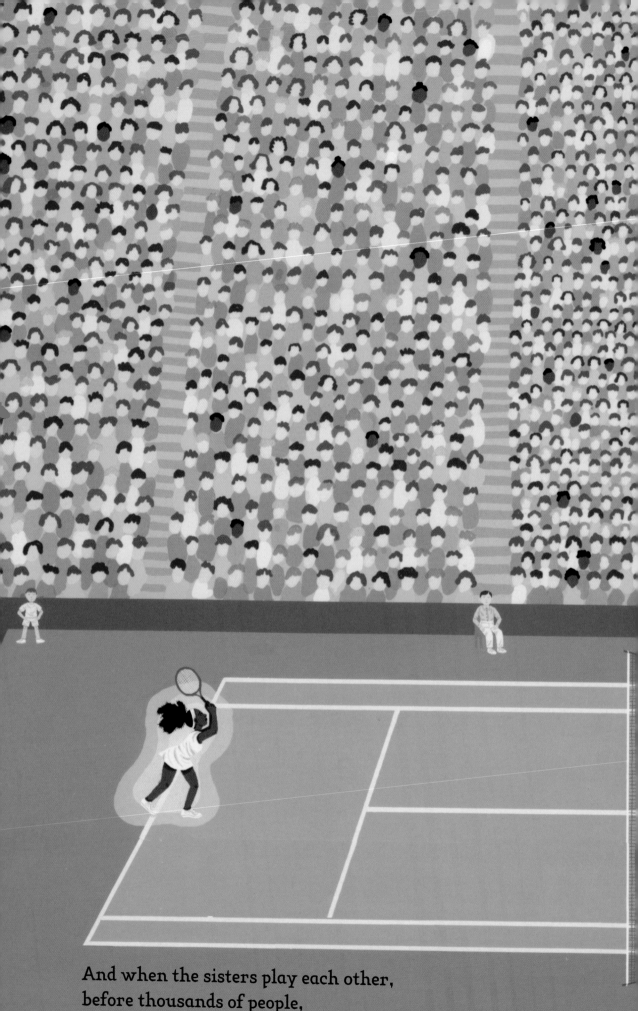

And when the sisters play each other,
before thousands of people,
that cocoon of concentration wraps around each of them.

It's like they're alone on the court.
Just like they were on the raggedy court in Compton—
spirits soaring high—together,

SISTERS.

Remembering Barbara   —J. W.

BIBLIOGRAPHY

Baird, Maiken, and Michelle Major, dirs. *Venus and Serena*. 2013. New York: Magnolia Pictures.

Di Palma, Joycelyn, dir. *E! True Hollywood Story*. Season 8, episode 31, "The Williams Sisters." Aired May 23, 2004, on E!

Gray, F. Gary, dir. *Straight Outta Compton*. 2015; Los Angeles: Universal Studios Home Entertainment, 2016. DVD, 147 minutes.

Huang, Andrew, dir. *Diary*. Season 7, episode 3, "Diary of Serena Williams." Aired May 22, 2002, on MTV.

"Serena and Venus Williams Playing at Ages 7 and 8." YouTube video, 7:28. Posted January 4, 2011, by "tennisministry." https://www.youtube.com/watch?v=8qnyi2phCpk.

Terry, Joseph C., dir. *The Oprah Winfrey Show*. Season 14, episode 171, "Venus & Serena Williams." Aired November 27, 2002, on ABC.

Trans World Sport. "11 and 12-Year-Old Venus & Serena Williams on Trans World Sport." YouTube video, 6:40. Posted December 10, 2012, https://www.youtube.com/watch?v=p31aGy_jD3E.

Williams, Richard, and Bart Davis. *Black and White: The Way I See It*. New York: Atria Books, 2014.

Williams, Venus. Interview by John McKenzie. *ABC Day One*. 1995.

Williams, Venus, and Serena Williams. *How to Play Tennis*. New York: DK Publishing, 2004.

BEACH LANE BOOKS
An imprint of Simon & Schuster Children's Publishing Division
1230 Avenue of the Americas, New York, New York 10020
Copyright © 2019 by Jeanette Winter
All rights reserved, including the right of reproduction in whole or in part in any form.
BEACH LANE BOOKS is a trademark of Simon & Schuster, Inc.
For information about special discounts for bulk purchases, please contact Simon & Schuster Special Sales at 1-866-506-1949 or business@simonandschuster.com.
The Simon & Schuster Speakers Bureau can bring authors to your live event. For more information or to book an event, contact the Simon & Schuster Speakers Bureau at 1-866-248-3049 or visit our website at www.simonspeakers.com.
Book design by Ann Bobco | The text for this book was set in Key LightOsF. | Manufactured in China
0119 SCP | First Edition
2 4 6 8 10 9 7 5 3 1
CIP data for this book is available from the Library of Congress.
ISBN 978-1-5344-3121-8
ISBN 978-1-5344-3122-5 (eBook)